CW00429466

may you know GOD'S ...

light
IN the deepest darkness

PSALM 27 VERSE 1

peace
IN the
fiercest
Storm

MARK 4 VERSES 35-41

love that never gives UP

1 CORINTHIANS 13 VERSES 7-8

Rest
that restores
your soul

PSALM 23 VERSES 1-3

HOPE
that brings
new purpose

JEREMIAH 29 VERSE 11

AND MAY THE LORD
BLESS you
and keep you
and give
you HIS
PEACE

NUMBERS 6 VERSES 24-26